I0554651

***

For My Dad

FOREWORD

In this busy, technological world, where social distance means interacting through apps and quick sound bites, it is hard to ground ourselves and find true connection. It is easy to forget that Nature is right outside and doesn't need to be scheduled.

This social distance bleeds into our human and animal interactions - heightening fear and anxiety. Take a moment to just breathe, pause, and reconnect your mind and heart. You, and everyone around you, including your animal companions, will reap the benefits of these quiet moments. Let this book be one of your moments.

Natalie Olden-Stahl DVM, CVA CVNN

CONTENTS

INTRODUCTION

"I am I because my little dog knows me"
- Gertrude Stein

***

Where traditional dog ownership has reigned for generations, P.I.V.O.T. challenges the status quo. This exploration utilizes a simple 5-word acronym to help shift your perspective, replacing the concept of owning a dog with the idea of nurturing a natural approach to a profound relationship.

PIVOT emerges as a revolutionary force, challenging the established norms. This transformative journey introduces a straightforward acronym that will redefine your perspective, replacing the notion of mere dog ownership with a profound and natural approach to nurturing a deeper connection. Welcome to the new era of canine companionship.

P - PERCEPTION

Shifting Perspectives -
Embracing a Dog-Human Relationship

***

I n a world where the concept of owning a dog has become deeply ingrained, it takes courage to challenge this conventional notion and embark on a journey that transforms the way you view these loyal companions. This opening chapter invites you to explore this transformational power of shifting your perspective from dog "ownership" to nurturing a meaningful "relationship". By doing so, you will uncover the profound impact this shift can have on enhancing your understanding and connection with every dog in your life.

Step 1: Acknowledging the Paradigm Shift

Before embarking on this transformative journey, it's crucial to acknowledge the paradigm shift you are about to embrace. Recognize that the traditional concept of "ownership" implies possession and control, whereas cultivating a "relationship" emphasizes mutual understanding, respect, and companionship. Fostering this fundamental difference will serve as the cornerstone of your new perspective.

Step 2: Reflecting on Language

Words hold immense power in shaping our thoughts and perceptions. Think for a moment about the language you use when referring to your canine companion. Try replacing possessive terms like "my dog", with phrases that emphasize companionship such as, "the dog in my life" or "canine companion". This small expressive adjustment is a gentle reminder of your commitment to nurturing an individual and respectful relationship.

Step 3: Embracing Mutual Learning Positive Affirmations

Shift your mindset from being the sole teacher to embracing a journey of mutual learning. Recognize that just as you engage with the dogs in your life, these devoted beings have valuable lessons to teach you as well. Approach interactions with curiosity, openness, and a willingness to understand their unique perspectives, preferences, and emotions.

Step 4: Fostering Empathy

Developing a strong sense of empathy is pivotal in building a meaningful relationship. Practice placing yourself in their paws, attempting to see the world through their eyes. Replace the notion that a dog wants attention to a dog seeks your connection. This practice enhances your ability to anticipate the unique needs of every dog, interpret their body language, and respond compassionately to their emotions.

Step 5: Prioritizing Communication

Effective communication is at the heart of any healthy relationship. Focus on honing your ability to understand and convey messages to each dog in your life through non-verbal cues, energy, gestures, and body language. As you sharpen these skills, you'll notice an increased partnership in your interactions and a more profound sense of connection.

Step 6: Nurturing Bond Through Activities

Engage in activities that strengthen your bond. Embark on shared adventures whether it's exploring nature trails, enjoying road trips, participating in training sessions, or simply spending time together. These shared experiences foster a sense of companionship and reinforce the idea that your dog/human relationship is built on shared moments, not managed chaos.

Step 7: Practicing Mindful Presence

Being, just being, requires redirecting your focus from managing a dog's choices to just being in the beauty of the present. Engage in mindful exercises that allow you to fully immerse yourself in the moment. Practice deep breathing, meditation, or simply sitting in stillness while observing their behavior. This mindful presence enhances your ability to truly connect and understand your beloved companion's needs.

Step 8: Embracing Unconditional Love

Finally, embrace the concept of unconditional love for the dog in front of you. Free your relationship from expectations and conditions, focusing instead on cherishing the unique qualities that make each and every dog a treasured soul. As you let go of notions of control and ownership, you create a space for a profound and lasting connection built on love, respect, and understanding.

***

B y embracing these transformative steps and shifting your perspective from "ownership" to "relationship," you embark on a journey of both self-discovery and mutual growth. As you open your heart and mind to the world of dog-human relationship, you'll find that your understanding deepens, your connection strengthens, and your connection with every dog in your life becomes a source of boundless joy and true enrichment.

1 - INTENTION

Setting the Intention for a Dog-Human Relationship

***

The power of intention lives in its ability to shape reality, directing energy towards a specific outcome. Open your mind to setting a meaningful intention for the dog-human relationship. By transforming your thoughts and sending the message that all the dogs in your life are healthy, balanced, and whole, you create a foundation for a purposeful connection.

Step 1: Embracing the Power of Intention

Before delving into the intricacies of intention, take a moment to appreciate its inherent power. Intention is more than a mere thought; it's a conscious decision to focus your energy and attention on a desired outcome. By recognizing the influence of intention, you open the door to creating a positive and transformative dog-human relationship.

Step 2: Shifting from Limiting Beliefs

Intention is a catalyst for change and transformation, and to set the desired intention, you must first examine and challenge any limiting beliefs you may hold about dogs. Release preconceived notions that dogs are solely dependent on us for every aspect. Instead, adopt the belief that dogs are inherently capable of balance, health, and purposeful living.

Step 3: Cultivating Positive Affirmations

Affirmations are a powerful tool for setting intention. Craft positive affirmations that reflect your vision of a dog-human relationship. Say these affirmations aloud daily, reinforcing the message that every dog in your life is healthy, balanced, and living their purpose. Over time, these affirmations become embedded in your subconscious, guiding your choices and interactions.

Step 4: Visualizing the Desired Outcome

Visualization is a technique that amplifies the power of intention. Give this try...close your eyes and vividly imagine each dog in your life radiating with vitality, exuding balance, and confidently embodying their purpose. Envision moments of ease, connection, and fulfillment shared between you and the dog in your life. As you visualize this desired outcome, you infuse it with intention and bring it closer to reality.

Step 5: Living with Mindful Awareness

Setting an intention is not a one-time act but a continuous practice. Cultivate mindful awareness of your thoughts, words, and actions in the context of your dog-human relationship. Whenever doubt or negativity arises, pause and redirect your focus to your intention. Make choices that align with the vision of a healthy, balanced, and purposeful dog.

Step 6: Nurturing Holistic Well-Being

Recognize that intention extends beyond physical well-being to encompass emotional, mental, and spiritual aspects. Commit to nurturing the holistic well-being for dogs in your life. Provide opportunities for physical exercise, mental stimulation, emotional connection, and moments of quiet contemplation. Embrace practices such as massage, energy work, and holistic therapies that contribute to their overall balance.

Step 7: Partnering with Your Dogs

Shift from the role of "owner" to that of a trusted partner. Approach every dog with respect and understanding that they too have their own journey. Invite open communication by paying attention to their cues, body language, and behavior. Create an environment where your intention of balance and wholeness is reflected in every interaction.

Step 8: Reflecting and Adapting

Regularly reflect on your intention and its impact on the dog-human relationship. Notice the changes in behavior, energy, and connection that arise from setting a meaningful intention. Adapt your approach as needed, fine-tuning your intention to align with the evolving needs and growth of both you and the dog in your life.

***

*B*y setting the intention that all the dogs in your life are healthy, balanced, and living their purpose, you are laying the groundwork for a transformative and meaningful relationship. As you infuse intention into your daily interactions, thoughts, and choices, you create an environment that fosters well-being, connection, and *mutual growth. The journey of setting intentions is an ongoing process, one that deepens your understanding of dogs and paves the way for a natural and purposeful bond.*

V - VALUE

Unveiling the Intrinsic Value of Each Dog

***

Unlock the profound value present within every dog. It is important to understand each dog's unique mind/body constitution or true nature, you will gain the insight needed to make enlightened decisions that honor their individuality and enhance your daily interactions.

Step 1: Embracing Individuality

Just as every human possesses a distinct personality and character, each dog embodies its own unique essence. Embrace the idea that each dog is an individual with their own preferences, needs, and qualities. Advance your perspective from viewing them as a collective species to celebrating the diversity that makes each dog special.

Step 2: Exploring the Mind/Body Constitution

A dog's mind/body constitution encompasses their physical, emotional, and energetic makeup. Every dog is different. Take the time to observe and analyze each dog in your life closely. Notice their physical attributes, such as body shape, coat texture, and eye color. Additionally, pay attention to their emotional traits, including temperament, reactions, and preferences. This comprehensive understanding forms the foundation for recognizing their intrinsic value.

Step 3: Unveiling Unique Qualities

Dive deeper into each dog's unique qualities. Reflect on their behaviors, playfulness, sociability, and interactions with other dogs and humans. Consider their preferences for activities, nutrition, types of play, and environments. The weather, noise levels, and moon cycles deeply affect each dog differently. Through this exploration, you will begin to uncover the distinctive gifts and attributes that contribute to their individuality.

Step 4: Honoring Needs and Desires

Understanding a dog's mind/body constitution enables you to meet their needs and honor their desires more effectively. Tailor your interactions, activities, and care routines to align with their specific constitution. What you find enjoyable may be the very opposite for the dog in front of you. Provide opportunities for mental and physical stimulation that resonate with their preferences, fostering a sense of fulfillment and well-being.

Step 5: Enhancing Daily Decisions

As you deepen your understanding of each dog's uniqueness, you will naturally make more informed and considerate decisions in your daily interactions. Whether it's selecting species-appropriate nutrition, designing enrichment activities, or choosing companions for socialization, your choices will reflect a conscious awareness of each dog s mind/body constitution.

Step 6: Embracing Holistic Wellness

Recognize that a dog's value extends beyond the physical realm to encompass emotional and energetic dimensions. Embrace holistic wellness practices that support their overall well-being. Engage in activities that promote mental stimulation, emotional connection, and energetic balance. By nurturing these aspects, you amplify the intrinsic value that each dog brings to your life.

Step 7: Fostering Connection

Understanding a dog's unique mind/body constitution deepens the bond of connection with each dog in your life. As you make choices to tailor your interactions to align with their individuality, you create an environment of trust, mutual respect, and understanding. This foundation of connection enriches your relationship and enhances the quality of your time together.

Step 8: Cultivating Gratitude

Recognize the privilege of sharing your life with a dog who houses their own distinct gifts and qualities. Cultivate gratitude for the opportunity to learn from their uniqueness and grow alongside them. Embrace the joy that arises from witnessing their individual traits and celebrating the value every dog infuses into your daily life.

Step 9: Sharing Uniqueness

Extend the practice of recognizing value beyond your own personal interactions with dogs. Share the stories of a dog's uniqueness with others, fostering a deeper appreciation for the diversity present within the canine world. By highlighting the individual qualities of each dog, you contribute to a collective understanding of the beauty and worth inherent in every canine companion.

***

Understanding each dog's unique mind/body constitution is a transformative journey that enriches your dog-human relationship. As you delve through the intricacies of their individuality, you uncover a treasure trove of value that shapes your interactions, decisions, and perspective. By embracing their distinct qualities, you create a natural and meaningful connection that honors the essence of each dog in your life.

O - OFFER

Embracing Unconditional Acceptance

***

What a wonderful offering to live within the profound practice of fully accepting each dog in your life, unburdened by expectations or judgments. By cultivating a space of unconditional acceptance, you create a nurturing environment that fosters trust, harmony and a deep connection with all the dogs in your life.

Step 1: Letting Go of Expectations

Begin by releasing any preconceived notions or expectations you may have about your dog. Recognize that each dog is a unique individual with their journey, abilities, and limitations. Free yourself from projecting desired outcomes onto them and embrace the beauty of allowing them to simply be themselves.

Step 2: Cultivating Present-Moment Awareness

Shift your focus to the present moment when interacting with a dog. Let go of concerns and worries about the past or future, and immerse yourself fully in the here and now. Engage in activities that encourage a sense of grounding such as mindful walks, silent observation, or meditative breathing. This practice creates a space where acceptance naturally flourishes.

Step 3: Non-Judgmental Observation

Observe dogs without attaching judgments or evaluations to their behaviors or actions. If you look for the negative, it will be found. Practice neutrality in your observations, allowing their natural expressions and responses to unfold without the filter of judgment. This enables you to connect with your dog on a deeper level, fostering a sense of safety and openness.

Step 4: Creating Silent Space

Designate moments of silent connection with each dog in your life. Find a peaceful setting where you can sit quietly together, without any external distractions. Gently gaze into their eyes, creating a silent dialogue that conveys your unconditional acceptance and presence. Allow the bond between you to deepen in the stillness.

Step 5: The Gift of Presence

Offer the precious gift of your undivided presence to a dog. Engage in activities that require minimal distractions, such as a peaceful nature walk or a quiet afternoon spent together. Demonstrate to the dog in your life that you are fully there for them, allowing them to feel cherished and valued for their authentic selves.

Step 6: Letting the Dog Lead

Allow the dog to make their own decisions. Choose to follow their cues, preferences, and pace, honoring their autonomy and choices. By relinquishing control and giving them the freedom to express themselves, you create an environment where they feel seen and accepted without reservation.

Step 7: Communicating Unconditional Love

Convey your unconditional acceptance through your actions, gestures, and touch. Engage in gentle petting, cuddling, and soothing words that communicate your love and appreciation for the dog exactly as they are. Let your touch be a testament to your unwavering support and connection.

Step 8: Liberating from Expectations

The practice of offering full acceptance liberates both you and the dog in your life from the weight of expectations. Embrace the freedom of allowing the dog to explore, learn, and grow at their own pace. This liberating approach enhances their confidence and encourages them to express their true selves.

Step 9: Nurturing Authentic Connection

Through the practice of unconditional acceptance, you nurture an authentic and profound connection with dogs in your life. By acknowledging their unique qualities, behaviors, and emotions without judgment, you create a safe haven where they can be their true selves. This authentic connection deepens your bond and enriches your relationship.

Step 10: The Power of "I Have No Expectations of You"

Embrace the transformative power of the statement, "I have no expectations of you." Utter these words with sincerity and intention, conveying your commitment to accepting every dog completely, without conditions. Let this affirmation serve as a reminder of your dedication to fostering a relationship built on genuine acceptance and unwavering love.

***

Cultivating the art of unconditional acceptance enriches your dog-human relationship in ways that transcend words. As you practice this profound form of connection regularly, you create a space where the dog can flourish, express themselves authentically, and thrive in the warmth of your unwavering acceptance.

T - THOUGHTFULNESS

The Thoughtful Path: Mindful Guardianship

***

We explore the importance of thoughtfulness in your interactions. By pausing, breathing, and approaching your role as a guardian with mindfulness, clarity, and consistency, you create a more harmonious environment that positively influences the dog's well-being and cultivates a deep sense of connection.

Step 1: Cultivating Mindful Awareness

Begin by cultivating mindful awareness of your thoughts, emotions, and actions in your interactions with the dog in your life. Pause and take a deep breath before engaging with your furry friend. Notice any impulses or reactions that arise within you and gently redirect your focus to the present moment.

Step 2: Clarity in Communication

As the guardian and partner, it is essential to communicate with clarity. Use clear verbal cues, body language, and physical energy to ensure that the dog in your life understands your expectations. Avoid mixed signals and be intentional in conveying your messages, developing a sense of security and understanding.

Step 3: Reflecting on Choices

Take moments to reflect on the choices you make in your interactions with every dog. Consider how your decisions impact their well-being, behavior, and emotions. Prioritize choices that promote their physical and emotional health, ensuring that your actions align with your commitment to their overall happiness.

Step 4: Creating a Calm Atmosphere

Establish a calm and peaceful atmosphere during your interactions. Avoid unnecessary distractions, loud noises, or sudden movements that may cause unease, anxiety, or stress for a dog. Set the tone for a serene environment that encourages relaxation, trust, and a deep connection.

Step 5: Consistency in Routine

Dogs thrive on routine, patterns, and predictability. Maintain a consistent daily routine for feeding, exercise, enrichment, and rest. Consistency provides a sense of stability and security, allowing a dog to anticipate their daily activities and establish a strong sense of trust in you as their guardian.

Step 6: Patience and Empathy

Practice patience and empathy as you navigate your dog-human relationship. Understand that each dog has their own unique pace of learning, adjusting, and responding. Be patient during training, behavioral challenges, and moments of uncertainty, and approach them with empathy and understanding.

Step 7: Attuning to Body Language

Develop a keen awareness of your dog's body language and signals. Pay attention to their expressions, posture, and movements to gain insights into their emotions and needs. This attunement enables you to respond appropriately and make decisions that prioritize their comfort and well-being.

Step 8: Mindful Play and Bonding

Engage in mindful play and bonding activities that strengthen your connection. Dedicate quality time to activities that bring joy and relaxation to both you and the dog in your life. Whether it's a leisurely walk, engaging in a favorite game, or simply cuddling, these moments deepen your bond and reinforce the positive energy you share.

Step 9: Adaptation and Flexibility

Stay open to adapting your approach based on the dog's evolving needs and preferences. Flexibility in your routines, training methods, and interactions allows you to meet each dog where they are and ensure that your decisions align with their well-being.

Step 10: Reflecting on the Journey

Set aside moments to reflect on the journey you are on together. Consider for yourself the progress made, the challenges overcome, and the growth you've experienced as a guardian. Celebrate the milestones, both big and small, and acknowledge the positive impact your thoughtful approach has on a dog's life.

***

*B*y embracing thoughtfulness in your role as a guardian, you create an environment of mindful connection, mutual understanding, and genuine care. This intentional approach enhances a dog's quality of life, strengthens your bond, and paves the way for a natural and fulfilling relationship built on trust and love.

QUICK CHECKLIST

Key Points to PIVOT

***

<u>Think Differently</u>

Shift your perspective from "ownership" to "dog-human relationship." Replace preconceived notions with a deep **understanding** and **appreciation** for each dog's unique personality and needs.

Offer Your Time

Dedicate meaningful time to spend with each of the dogs in your life. Immerse yourself in **the present moment**, observe their behaviors individually, and enjoy the experience of connecting with them.

Learn Canine Language

Develop the ability to interpret canine body language. **Recognize signs** of happiness, sadness, tiredness, contentment, nervousness, and fear. Use this insight to guide your decisions and interactions.

Communicate Concisely

Practice clear and mindful communication with the dogs in your life. Pause, breathe, and **maintain consistency** in your cues and actions. Understand that dogs keenly observe your movements and energy.

Enrichment Through Play

Engage in **playful activities** to strengthen your bond and connection. Play is a powerful tool for learning and building relationships. Explore various activities that cater to each dog's preferences and provide opportunities for growth and connection.

UP PLAN

Urgent Pet (UP) Plan

***

As we extend our focus beyond ourselves during times of crisis and disaster, reaching out to others and ensuring their well-being, let us also extend the same care and consideration to our beloved animals. One way to do this is to create an UP plan for their care in the event that you are ill, in the midst of trauma, hospitalized, or untimely deceased.

Here are THREE TIPS for consideration:

1) Designate a Care Team

Designate two or three people that will work together as a "Care Team". Timelines can be unpredictable. Also making decisions regarding your animals. Be sure that they know your wishes and are prepared to care for your beloved animals for as long as needed.

Reach out to your preferred designates RIGHT NOW. Have a very real and honest conversation and ask for their commitment to you and to your beloved animals.

Consider an addendum to your legal documents specifying your instructions and designated funds regarding potential Long-term Care, Veterinary 24-hour Contact Telephone and Location and ALL Caretakers' Contact Information.

2) Create an Urgent Pet Plan Supply Kit

The **UP-Plan Supply Kit** is to contain items for a minimum of TWO WEEKS.

•Typed Daily Care Instructions

•Current Copy of Medical Records (Recent Vaccinations, Microchip ID# and Veterinarian Contact Information)

•Names/Contact Information for All Caretakers including Other Potential Back-Up Designates

•Crate, Carrier, Seatbelt Attachment, Bed, Blanket for Transport

•Medications/Supplements with Dosages and Instructions

•Food, Bowls, Treats, Leash, Harness, Favorite Toys and Other Supplies

•T-shirts, a Pillowcase, or Clothing Items Placed in Separate Resealable Bags. Your scent provides comfort for your beloved animals.

3) UP Plan Information Availability

Place **Urgent Pet Information** on Your Person in TWO Locations:

•Directly Behind or Near Your Driver's License or ID Card

•Mobile Phone within Your Contact Card and Show Medical ID information

Also, place UP-PLAN Caretakers Information and Statement on your Desktop, Tablet/Laptop Chargers and Landline Phone

The **UP-PLAN Statement** may include:

"I HAVE ANIMALS IN MY HOME! Please contact _____ at Telephone #_____ and Email Address_____.

In addition, contact _____ at Telephone # _____ and Email Address _____."

ABOUT THE AUTHOR

Tina Makris, an educator, dog behaviorist, and musician, embodies unwavering compassion. Settled in the tranquil embrace of Arizona's Superstition Mountains, she shares her journey with her wife. This pocketbook guide draws from Tina's deep belief in Ayurvedic principles and the profound love that intertwines with the lives of every canine companion she has known or has yet to know.